Strawberry & Cracker
TWINS WITH FETAL ALCOHOL SYNDROME

THE SCHOOL DAY

Story by Barbara Studham   Illustrated by Heather Lamb

ISBN: 978-1-988092-08-9

INTRODUCTION

Fetal Alcohol Syndrome (FAS) is a diagnosis within the range of Fetal Alcohol Spectrum Disorders (FASD); a term defining the permanent birth defects and complex behaviors caused by prenatal exposure to alcohol.

Strawberry and Cracker are twins with Fetal Alcohol Syndrome who live with their grandma and her dog, Thunder. With over twenty years of experience parenting grandchildren with FAS, I created the series through my perception of the disorder.

THE SCHOOL DAY describes a school day for children with FAS receiving support from the school, teachers, and their grandma. Support that includes the use of visual aids, attending a special needs class, and help from an educational assistant and school friends who understand daily life with a disability.

Despite the support, after-school hours can bring stress, so grandma oversees the twins while they play with their school friends, and helps with their anxiety at night.

Barbara Studham

Strawberry & Cracker are twins. They have blond hair, and blue eyes. They were also born with Fetal Alcohol Syndrome.

The twins live with their grandma and her dog, Thunder.

Despite their disorder, Strawberry and Cracker have many strengths. Strawberry loves to sing and dance.

Cracker speeds on
his skateboard.

MORNING

SHOWER

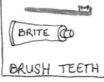

BRUSH TEETH

WEAR PULL-UP

GET DRESSED

BRUSH HAIR

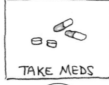

TAKE MEDS

Why do I have to brush my teeth?

I hate taking showers!

But, for a successful day, the twins rely on supports. Before school, they check their visual aid to see what comes next.

After breakfast, Strawberry and Cracker fetch their backpacks then wait on the porch for the school bus to arrive. The twins attend a special needs class with their friends, Mia, Jay, and Beck.

When in school, Strawberry and Cracker find the work difficult. Their class educational assistant, Ms. B., helps the twins when they get stuck.

When Strawberry grows anxious, Ms. B. takes her for a walk in the school grounds. But, Strawberry is not happy. She wants to go home.

When the twins return home, after-school stress makes them act out. Seeing bubbles in the kitchen sink, Cracker douses his sister. Strawberry fights back!

Beck, Mia, and Jay, arrive at the house to play basketball with the twins. Grandma pushes Beck to the park while he holds Thunder's leash.

Strawberry jumps onto Cracker who speeds off to the park.

Mia and Jay are getting impatient. Grandma asks the twins to play nicely. She knows if the twins won't share, their friends will leave.

NIGHT

SHOWER

BRITE
BRUSH TEETH

WEAR PULL-UP

WEAR PYJAMAS

TAKE MEDS

BEDTIME STORY

I'll choose the bedtime story.

We need to take our meds.

After supper, the twins check their nighttime visual aid before preparing for bedtime.

When the twins are prepared for bed, Grandma reads them a story. She hopes it will calm the twins before bedtime. But, the twins don't fall asleep easily.

When in bed, Cracker grows anxious. Falling asleep is never easy. He calls to Grandma for his favorite toy rabbit. He hopes his toy will relax him and help him sleep.

Strawberry is scared of the dark. She imagines a monster under her bed. Her anxiety is making it hard for her to sleep.

Grandma brings Cracker his favorite toy rabbit. She also brings his truck and baseball. With his toys at his side, Cracker finally falls asleep.

Strawberry relaxes with her music, and snuggles with Thunder. With her night light glowing, she hopes to forget the monster under her bed and fall asleep.

Goodnight, Strawberry!
Goodnight, Cracker!

This book is dedicated to people who
support children with an FASD.

FIDGET! All children fidget, but children with Fetal Alcohol Syndrome often over-fidget, thereby annoying people unaware of the disorder. By discussing strategies, the twins' caregiver grandma hopes the calming methods will lessen the twins' fidgeting.

THE SCHOOL DAY features the twins' use of visual aids, their attendance in a special needs class, their daily struggle with anxiety, learning, and sensory issues, and the supports required for a successful day.

THE BIRTHDAY BASH. The noise and liveliness associated with parties can overwhelm a child with Fetal Alcohol Syndrome and result in misbehavior or meltdowns.

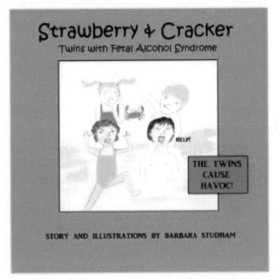

THE TWINS CAUSE HAVOC! Taking children with Fetal Alcohol Syndrome on a trip can be challenging. At the beach, the twins anger parents and vendors, but escape their clutches by jumping off the pier and into the churning sea!

THE MELTDOWN. While shopping for new shoes, Strawberry has a meltdown. Cracker throws a tantrum when Grandma tells him they have to leave the store.

THE TWINS' SENSORY SMARTS. Strawberry and Cracker are challenged by sensory disorders. With Grandma's help they have found ways to cope.

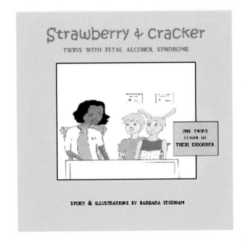

ADVOCATE! On Fetal Alcohol Awareness Day, Grandma encourages the twins to advocate by sharing their FASD feelings with the community.

THE TWINS LEARN OF THEIR DISORDER. After an evaluation, the twins learn they have Fetal Alcohol Syndrome. Their doctor offsets their panic through a calm and positive discussion.

THE STRAWBERRY & CRACKER SERIES IS AVAILABLE FROM AMAZON

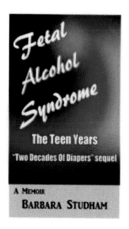

TWO DECADES OF DIAPERS. During, author, Barbara Studham's twenty years single-handedly raising four grandchildren with Fetal Alcohol Syndrome, her temptation to run from this often uncontrollable disorder was significant. Eventually overwhelming her parental abilities the disorder finally caused a breakdown of the family unit she had tried so hard to maintain.

FETAL ALCOHOL SYNDROME, THE TEEN YEARS. This sequel gives insight into the challenges and struggles Barbara Studham experienced while raising teens with Fetal Alcohol Syndrome. Here, she relates the whirlwind of emotions and trauma caused by FAS during that time.

ABOUT THE AUTHOR

For over twenty years Barbara Studham has parented grandchildren with Fetal Alcohol Syndrome (FAS). Motivated by her experience, she created the children's FASD picture book series titled, Strawberry & Cracker, Twins with Fetal Alcohol Syndrome. Designed for children ages 5-12, currently available in the series are: THE SCHOOL DAY, FIDGET!, ADVOCATE!, THE TWINS LEARN OF THEIR DISORDER, THE BIRTHDAY BASH, THE TWINS CAUSE HAVOC, THE MELTDOWN, and THE TWINS' SENSORY SMARTS.

Barbara also wrote two FASD memoirs relating to her years raising grandchildren with Fetal Alcohol Syndrome. TWO DECADES OF DIAPERS describes how she became a grandma raising grandchildren, and the challenges she faced when the children were young. FETAL ALCOHOL SYNDROME, THE TEEN YEARS describes her emotional journey while dealing with the complex behaviours associated with her grandchildren's adolescence.

Barbara has also written fiction, including the six-book English seaside series UNDER THE SHANKLIN SKY, THE BATHING BEAUTY, THE FARING FOXGLOVE, MANN OVERBOARD, THE SPITTING IMAGE, and, A HINT OF SPRING. All Barbara's books are available from AMAZON.

BOOKS by Barbara Studham

MEMOIRS

Two Decades of Diapers

Fetal Alcohol Syndrome, The Teen Years

Psychopathetic

CHILDREN'S FASD BOOKS

The School Day

Fidget!

Advocate!

The Twins Learn Of Their Disorder

The Birthday Bash

The Twins Cause Havoc!

The Meltdown

The Twins' Sensory Smarts

FICTION

Friday at 4:00

The Look of a Twelve-year-old

Not My Type

ENGLISH SEASIDE SERIES

Under The Shanklin Sky

The Bathing Beauty

The Faring Foxglove

A Hint of Spring

The Spitting Image

Mann Overboard

Made in the USA
Monee, IL
06 February 2021